A Little Jazz Mass

Bob Chilcott

for upper voices, piano, and optional bass and drum kit

Vocal score

MUSIC DEPARTMENT

OXFORD
UNIVERSITY PRESS

OXFORD
UNIVERSITY PRESS

Great Clarendon Street, Oxford OX2 6DP,
United Kingdom

Oxford University Press is a department of the University of Oxford.
It furthers the University's objective of excellence in research, scholarship,
and education by publishing worldwide. Oxford is a registered trade mark of
Oxford University Press in the UK and in certain other countries

First published 2004

ISBN 978-0-19-343328-1

Music origination by Jeanne Roberts
Printed in Great Britain on acid-free paper by
Halstan & Co. Ltd., Amersham, Bucks.

Contents

1. Kyrie   5

2. Gloria   9

3. Sanctus   15

4. Benedictus   17

5. Agnus Dei   20

Composer's note

A Little Jazz Mass was written for the massed choirs of the 2004 Crescent City Choral Festival, and first performed in St Louis Cathedral, New Orleans in June of that year.

I have always loved jazz. At the beginning of my writing career I worked from time to time as an arranger for the now defunct BBC Radio Orchestra and, while a member of the King's Singers, I was lucky enough to perform with such artists as George Shearing, Richard Rodney Bennett, John Dankworth, Art Farmer, and the WDR Big Band. These experiences and influences have all had an impact on the music that I compose.

In this mass setting I have written a piano part which may be played exactly as written. However, I would encourage the pianist to improvise freely on the chord structure, and would also encourage the addition of bass and drums and any other instruments that may be appropriate for the performance.

I am grateful to Cheryl Dupont, the conductor of the New Orleans Children's Chorus, for enabling this work to come to life in such a great jazz city, and to all the children in the Crescent City Choral Festival Choir 2004, who gave it such a great start. I am also grateful to Neil Richardson, a wonderful musician who, more than twenty years ago, gave me my first opportunity as a professional arranger at the BBC.

Duration: *c.*12 minutes

Commissioned by Cheryl Dupont and the New Orleans Children's Chorus
for the 2004 Crescent City Choral Festival

A Little Jazz Mass

1. *Kyrie*

BOB CHILCOTT

* The piano part can be played as written or used as a guide. Bass and drum kit can join *ad lib.*

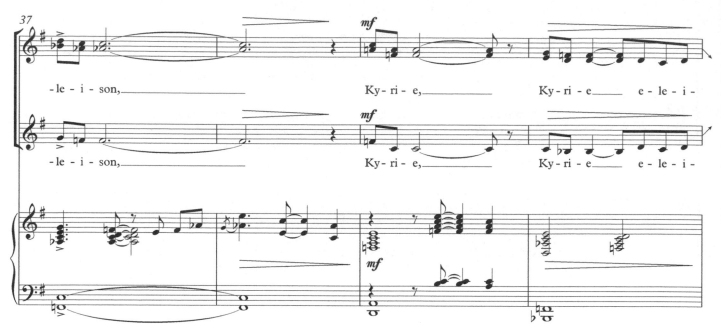

-le - i - son, _____ Ky - ri - e, _____ Ky - ri - e ___ e - le - i-

-le - i - son, _____ Ky - ri - e, _____ Ky - ri - e e - le - i-

TUTTI VOICES *unis.*

S.1 & 2
A.

- son. _____ Ky - ri - e, _____ Ky - ri -

poco rit.

- e, _____ Ky - ri - e e - le - i - son.

attacca

2. Gloria

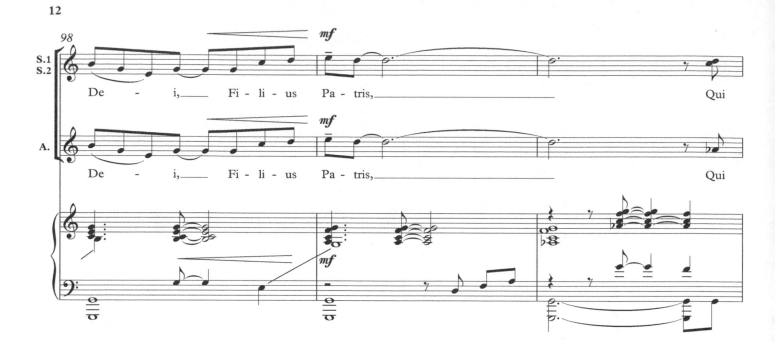

susci - pe de - pre - ca - ti - o - nem__ no - stram. Qui se - des ad dex - te - ram Pa -

susci - pe de - pre - ca - ti - o - nem__ no - stram. Qui se - des ad dex - te - ram Pa -

\- tris,_____ mi - se - re - re, mi - se - re - re__ no - bis._____

\- tris,_____ mi - se - re, mi - se - re - re no - bis.

(*pick up in new tempo*)

114 **Tempo I** ♩ = *c.*208

TUTTI VOICES *unis.* *f*

S.1 & 2
A.

Quo - ni - am Tu__ so - lus san - ctus,

quo - ni - am,   Quo - ni - am Tu___ so - lus san - ctus, quo - ni - am,

Tu so - lus,   so - lus Do - mi - nus, Tu so - lus Al - tis - si - mus,

Je - - su Chri - ste,   Je - su Chri - ste,

Je - su Chri - ste,   Cum San - cto, San - cto Spi - ri - tu in

glo - ri - a De - i Pa - tris, A - men, A - men.

3. Sanctus

San - ctus,_____ San - ctus Do-mi-nus,_____ San - ctus,

San - ctus,_____ San - ctus Do-mi-nus,_____ San - ctus,

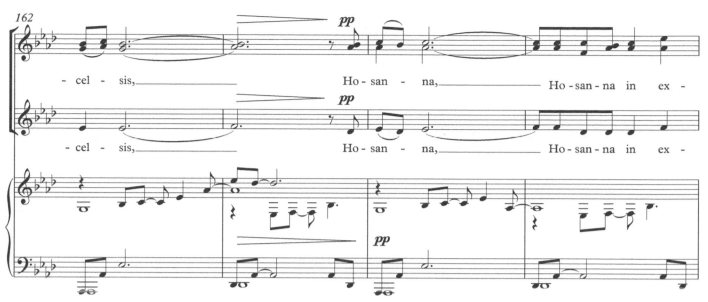

- cel - sis,＿＿＿＿＿＿ Ho - san - na,＿＿＿＿＿＿ Ho - san - na in ex -

- cel - sis,＿＿＿＿＿ Ho - san - na,＿＿＿＿＿ Ho - san - na in ex -

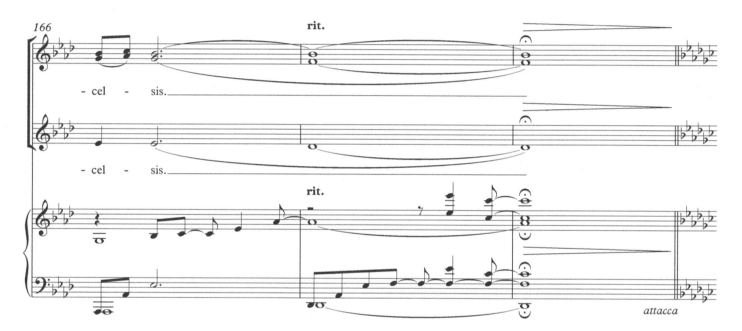

- cel - sis.＿＿＿＿＿＿＿＿＿＿＿

- cel - sis.＿＿＿＿＿

attacca

4. *Benedictus*

-san - na in ex - cel - sis, in ex - cel - sis._____

-san - na in ex - cel - sis, in ex - cel - sis._____

-san - na in ex - cel - sis, in ex - cel - sis._____

ff

attacca

for Richard and Catherine Webber

5. *Agnus Dei*

Bluesy feel ♩ = c.63

S.1 & 2
A.

p

TUTTI VOICES *unis.*
mp espress.

A - gnus De - i, A - gnus De - i,_____ qui

mp

*If playing this movement with bass, the first four bars should be played as a piano solo, with the bass entering at bar 203.

*If playing with bass, omit the piano left hand in bars 219–222 to allow a bass solo. The left hand re-enters at bar 223.

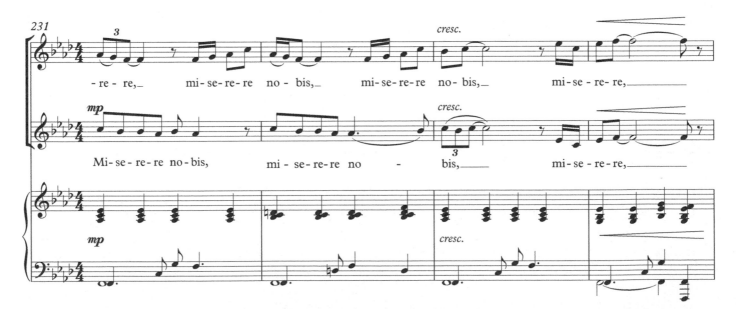

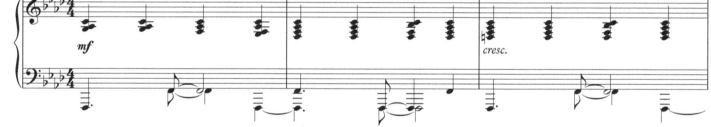

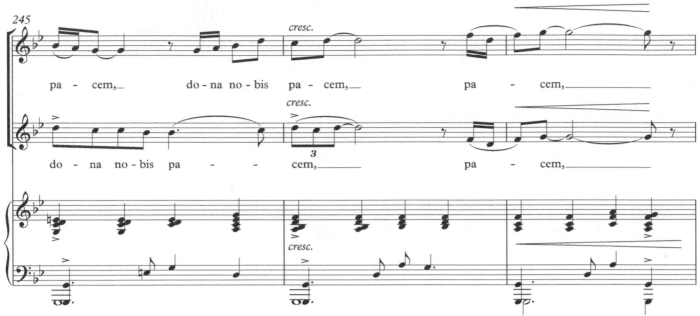

Printed in England by Halstan & Co. Ltd., Amersham, Bucks.